GRAND CANYON NATIONAL PARK ACTIVITY BOOK

PUZZLES, MAZES, GAMES, AND MORE ABOUT GRAND CANYON NATIONAL PARK

NATIONAL PARKS ACTIVITIES SERIES

GRAND CANYON NATIONAL PARK ACTIVITY BOOK

Copyright 2021
Published by Little Bison Press

For more free national parks activities, visit
www.littlebisonpress.com

Table of Contents

About the Grand Canyon 4
Where is the Park? 5
Who Lives Here? 7
Visitor's Log 9
Common Names vs. Scientific Names 10
The Ten Essentials 13
Connect the Dots #1 14
Photobook 15
Grand Canyon Bingo 16
Things To Do Jumble 17
Maze: Birdwatching 18
Camping Packing List 19
Connect the Dots #2 20
Listen Carefully 21
Grand Canyon Wordsearch 22
What are Baby Animals Called? 23
Mad Libs: The Perfect Picnic Spot 24
Maze: Hike to Havasupai Falls 26
Word Search: Phantom Ranch 27
Leave No Trace Quiz 28
Park Poetry 29
Maze: Rafting the Colorado 30
Stacking Rocks 31
Crack the Code 32
Crossword: The Land of the Havasupai 33
Maze: Canyon Mule Ride 34
Butterflies of the Grand Canyon 35
Mad Libs: A Hike at the Grand Canyon 36
Word Search: Let's Go Camping 38
All in the Day of a Park Ranger 39
Draw Yourself as a Park Ranger 40
Rattlesnakes of the Grand Canyon 41
Amphibians 42
Other National Parks 44
Answer Key 46

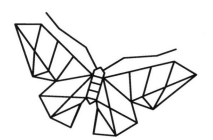
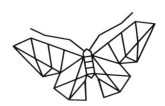

About Grand Canyon National Park

Grand Canyon National Park is located in northern Arizona. It is home to the immense Grand Canyon. Layered bands of red rocks make millions of years of geological history easy to see. Over millions of years, the Colorado River carved through the rock and made the deep ravine that exists today. The arid landscape of this region is host to cacti, the critically endangered California Condor, and a diverse range of desert wildlife.

This park receives millions of visitors every year. It receives the second most visitors of all US National Parks, surpassed only by Great Smoky Mountains National Park.

Famous for:
- mule trains
- the scenic gorge
- rafting on the Colorado River
- unique geologic features

> Hey, I'm Parker!
>
> I'm the only snail in history to visit every National Park in the United States! Come join me on my adventures in Grand Canyon National Park.
>
> Throughout this book, we will learn about the history of the park, the animals and plants that live here, and things to do if you ever visit in person. This book is also full of games and activities!
>
> Last but not least, I am hidden 9 times on different pages. See how many times you can find me. This page doesn't count!

Where is the Park?

Grand Canyon National Park is in the southwest United States. It is located in northern Arizona. Out of all the national parks in the US, the Grand Canyon has the second most annual visitors.

Arizona

Look at the shape of Arizona. Can you find it on the map? If you are from the US, can you find your home state? Color Arizona red. Put a star on the map where you live.

Javelina look like pigs, but they are not pigs. They are sometimes called collared peccary or musk hogs.

Mountain lions live in the forests of the North and South Rims of the canyon.

Who Lives Here?

Here are eleven plants and animals that live in the park.
Use the word bank to fill in the clues below.

word bank: javelina, mountain lion, ringtail, condor, falcon, gila monster, rattlesnake, tarantula, utah yucca, burrobush, salt cedar

The California Condor is one of the rarest birds in the world. They were almost extinct, but conservation efforts have helped increase their population numbers.

Bighorn Sheep are the largest animals native to the park. Elk and bison are larger, but they are not native to the Grand Canyon. Rather, those species were introduced to the ecosystem by humans.

Grand Canyon National Park

Visitor's Log

Date: _____ Season: _____

Who I went with: _____ Which entrance: _____

How was your experience? Write a few sentences about your trip. Where did you stay? What did you do? What was your favorite activity? If you haven't visited the park yet, write a paragraph pretending that you did.

_____
_____
_____
_____
_____

STAMPS

Many national parks and monuments have cancellation stamps for visitors to use. These rubber stamps record the date and location that you visited. Many people collect the markings as a free souvenir. Check with a ranger to see where you can find a stamp during your visit. If you aren't able to find one, you can draw your own.

Common Names
vs.
Scientific Names

A common name of an organism is a name that is based on everyday language. You have heard the common names of plants, animals, and other living things on tv, in books, and at school. Common names can also be referred to as "English" names, popular names, or farmer's names. Common names can vary from place to place. The word for a particular tree may be one thing, but that same tree has a different name in another country. Common names can even vary from region to region, even in the same country.

Scientific names, or Latin names, are given to organisms to make it possible to have uniform names for the same species. Scientific names are in Latin. You may have heard plants or animals referred to by their scientific name or parts of their scientific names. Latin names are also called "binomial nomenclature," which refers to a two-part naming system. The first part of the name – the generic name – refers to the genus to which the species belongs. The second part of the name, the specific name, identifies the species. For example, Tyrannosaurus rex is an example of a widely known scientific name.

COMMON NAME

Elk
Cervus canadensis

Hognose Skunk
Conepatus leuconotus

LATIN NAME = GENUS + SPECIES

Elk = Cervus canadensis

Hognose Skunk = Conepatus leuconotus

Find the Match!
Common Names and Latin Names

Match the common name to the scientific name for each animal. The first one is done for you. Use clues on the page before and after this one to complete the matches.

Elk   Pecari tajacu

Javelina   Conepatus leuconotus

Pileated Woodpecker   Rubus idaeus

Hog-nosed Skunk   Anaxyrus cognatus

Great Horned Owl   Gymnogyps californianus

California Condor   Crotalus viridis nuntius

Desert Prickly Pear   Bubo virginianus

Red Raspberry   Cervus canadensis

Great Plains Toad   Dryocopus pileatus

Hopi Rattlesnake   Opuntia engelmannii

11

Desert Prickly Pear
Opuntia engelmannii

California Condor
Gymnogyps californianus

Red Raspberry
Rubus idaeus

Some plants and animals who live in the Grand Canyon

Great Horned Owl
Bubo virginianus

Hopi Rattlesnake
Crotalus viridis nuntius

Great Plains Toad
Anaxyrus cognatus

12

The Ten Essentials

The ten essentials are a list of things that are important to have when you go for longer hikes. If you go on a hike to the <u>backcountry</u>, it is especially important that you have everything you need in case of an emergency. If you get lost or something unforeseen happens, it is good to be prepared to survive until help finds you.

The ten essentials list was developed in the 1930s by an outdoors group called the Mountaineers. Over time and technological advancements, this list has evolved. Can you identify all the things on the current list? Circle each of the "essentials" and cross out everything that doesn't make the cut.

fire: matches, lighter, tinder, and/or stove	a pint of milk	extra money	headlamp plus extra batteries	extra clothes
extra water	a dog	Polaroid camera	bug net	lightweight games, such as a deck of cards
extra food	a roll of duct tape	shelter	sun protection such as sunglasses, sun-protective clothes, and sunscreen	knife, plus a gear repair kit
a mirror	navigation: map, compass, altimeter, GPS device, or satellite messenger	first aid kit	extra flip-flops	entertainment, such as video games or books

Backcountry - a remote undeveloped rural area.

Connect the Dots #1

This animal lives in almost every state in the US, including Grand Canyon National Park. They are nocturnal, more active at night, and sleep during the day. They are omnivorous eaters, meaning they eat both plants and animals.

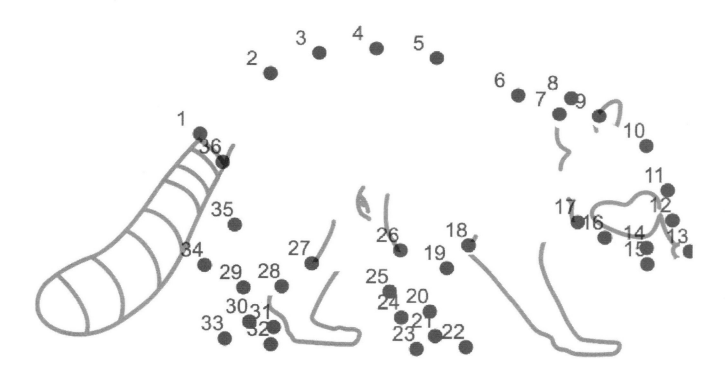

Are you an omnivore like a raccoon? An herbivore only eats plant foods. A carnivore only eats meat. An omnivore eats both. What type of eater are you? Write down some of your favorite foods to back up your answer.

_____

_____

Photobook

Draw some pictures of things you saw in the park.

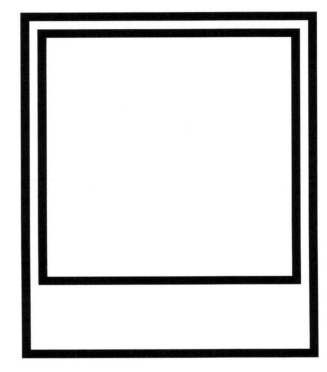
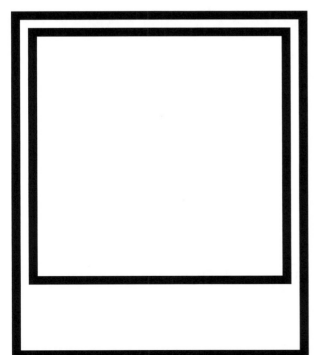
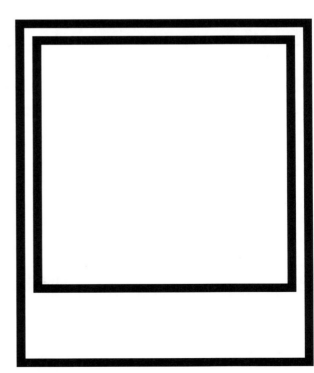

Grand Canyon Bingo

Let's play bingo! Cross off each box you are able to during your visit to the national park. Try to get a bingo down, across, or diagonally. If you can't visit the park, use the bingo board to plan your perfect trip.

Pick out some activities you would want to do during your visit. What would you do first? How long would you spend there? What animals would you try to see?

RIDE A MULE	GO RAFTING	IDENTIFY A TREE	TAKE A PICTURE AT AN OVERLOOK	WATCH A MOVIE AT THE VISITORS CENTER
GO FOR A HIKE	SPOT OTHER PEOPLE RIDING MULES	CLIMB THE STONE WATCHTOWER	LEARN ABOUT THE INDIGENOUS PEOPLE WHO LIVE IN THIS AREA	VISIT THE NORTH RIM
SEE THE COLORADO RIVER	VISIT THE SOUTH RIM	FREE SPACE	SPOT THE GRAND CANYON RAILWAY	VISIT A RANGER STATION
PICK UP A PIECE OF TRASH	WITNESS A SUNRISE OR SUNSET AT THE CANYON EDGE	SEE A BIGHORN SHEEP	GO CAMPING	SPOT A BIRD OF PREY
LEARN ABOUT THE GEOLOGY OF THE CANYON	CLIMB DOWN THE CANYON	HAVE A PICNIC	SPOT SOME ANIMAL TRACKS	PARTICIPATE IN A RANGER-LED ACTIVITY

Things To Do Jumble

Unscramble the letters to uncover activities you can do while in Grand Canyon National Park. Hint: each one ends in -ing.

1. RATF ☐☐☐☐ING

2. KHI ☐☐☐ING

3. RDIB ☐☐☐☐ING

4. MACP ☐☐☐☐ING

5. KINCIPC ☐☐☐☐☐☐☐ING

6. EISSTEHG ☐☐☐☐☐☐☐☐ING

7. MRIDULE ☐☐☐☐☐☐☐ING

Word Bank

birding
reading
camping
muleriding
skiing
rafting
hunting
singing
yelling
sightseeing
picnicking
hiking
skateboarding

17

Go Birdwatching for the California Condor

start here

DID YOU KNOW? The California Condor almost went extinct? In 1982, there were less than 30 California Condors left in the world.

Camping Packing List

What should you take with you when you go camping? Pretend you are in charge of your family camping trip. Make a list of what you would need to be safe and comfortable on an overnight excursion. Some considerations are listed on the side.

1.
2.
3.
4.
5.
6.
7.
8.
9.
10.
11.
12.
13.
14.
15.
16.

- What will you eat at every meal?
- What will the weather be like?
- Where will you sleep?
- What will you do during your free time?
- How luxurious do you want camp to be?
- How will you cook?
- How will you see at night?
- How will you dispose of trash?
- What might you need in case of emergencies?

Connect the Dots #2

California Condors have the largest wingspan of any other bird in North America. Condors have wingspans of up to eleven feet! A wingspan is the distance from one wingtip to the other wingtip. There is a similar measurement for humans. This is called an arm span, since humans don't have wings.

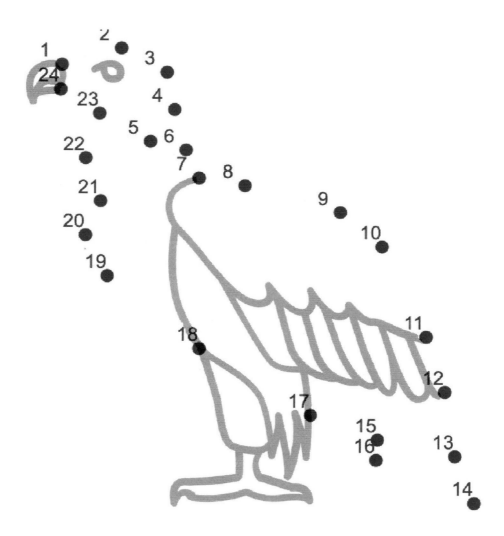

Do you know how long your arm span is? You can have a friend or family member help you measure it. Stand with your back against a wall and stretch out your arms. With a measuring tape, measure from the tip of your left middle finger to the tip of your right middle finger. How long is your arm span? Is it longer or shorter than the wingspan of a California Condor?

_____

_____

LISTEN CAREFULLY

Visitors to Grand Canyon National Park may hear different noises from those they hear at home. Try this activity to experience this for yourself!

First, find a place outside where it is comfortable to sit or stand for a few minutes. You can do this by yourself or with a friend or family member. Once you have a good spot, close your eyes and listen. Be quiet for one minute and pay attention to what you are hearing. List some of the sounds you have heard in one of the two boxes below:

NATURAL SOUNDS
MADE BY ANIMALS, TREES OR PLANTS, THE WIND, ETC

HUMAN-MADE SOUNDS
MADE BY PEOPLE, MACHINES, ETC

ONCE YOU ARE BACK AT HOME, TRY REPEATING YOUR EXPERIMENT:

NATURAL SOUNDS
MADE BY ANIMALS, TREES OR PLANTS, THE WIND, ETC

HUMAN-MADE SOUNDS
MADE BY PEOPLE, MACHINES, ETC

WHERE DID YOU HEAR MORE NATURAL SOUNDS? _____

WHERE DID YOU HEAR MORE HUMAN SOUNDS? _____

Grand Canyon Word Search

Words may be horizontal, vertical, diagonal, or they might be backwards!

1. Arizona
2. Colorado River
3. bats
4. condor
5. Hopi
6. deep
7. rodents
8. Navajo
9. mule
10. rafting
11. Havasupai
12. fungi
13. Paiute
14. Hualapai
15. rapids
16. geology
17. helicopters
18. erosion
19. South Rim
20. North Rim

```
C C I L H A V A S U P A I W F
H O A T D E E P S H E R W U J
T N L R K A O A C C L B N P B
S D P O S P R I A E R G U M C
C O A I R R R U Q N I U J K L
D R R L Y A O T D H O P I C I
E O A O P R D E A M B Z I A N
P H C G D H I O G W E I I X A
M U L E G E L O R E E D S R V
E A I O A L N Y H I N G O T A
S L A L A I S T A B V E N S J
S A N O K C O I S M O E I D O
I P O G F O I N O R T H R I M
O A G Y L P V E S O O R V P O
N I G N I T F A R S R O H A M
X J T F I E E F L I E S Q R E
U A E E E R O S I O N P V E B
C J D O S S O U T H R I M A S
```

22

Find the Match!
What are Baby Animals Called?

Match the animal to its baby. The first one is done for you.

Elk   chick

California Condor   calf

Canyon Bat   snakelets

Hog-nosed Skunk ⟶   pup

Great Horned Owl   owlet

Great Plains Toad   kit

Mountain Lion   tadpole

Hopi Rattlesnake   kitten

The Perfect Picnic Spot

Fill in the blanks on this page without looking at the full story. Once you have each line filled out, use the words you've chosen to complete the story on the next page.

- EMOTION _____
- FOOD _____
- SOMETHING SWEET _____
- STORE _____
- MODE OF TRANSPORTATION _____
- NOUN _____
- SOMETHING ALIVE _____
- SAUCE _____
- PLURAL VEGETABLES _____
- ADJECTIVE _____
- PLURAL BODY PART _____
- ANIMAL _____
- PLURAL FRUIT _____
- PLACE _____
- SOMETHING TALL _____
- COLOR _____
- ADJECTIVE _____
- NOUN _____
- A DIFFERENT ANIMAL _____
- FAMILY MEMBER #1 _____
- FAMILY MEMBER #2 _____
- VERB THAT ENDS IN -ING _____
- A DIFFERENT FOOD _____

The Perfect Picnic Spot

Use the words from the previous page to complete a silly story.

When my family suggested having our lunch at the Yaki Point picnic area, I was

_____. I love eating my _____ outside! I knew we had picked up a
EMOTION   FOOD

box of _____ from the _____ for after lunch, my favorite. We drove up
SOMETHING SWEET   STORE

to the area and I jumped out of the _____. "I will find the perfect spot for
                                   MODE OF TRANSPORTATION

a picnic!" I grabbed a _____ for us to sit on, and I ran off. I passed a picnic
                      NOUN

table, but it was covered with _____ so we couldn't sit there. The next
                              SOMETHING ALIVE

picnic table looked okay, but there were smears of _____ and pieces of
                                                   SAUCE

_____ everywhere. The people that were there before must have been
PLURAL VEGETABLES

_____! I gritted my _____ together and kept walking down the path,
ADJECTIVE   PLURAL BODY PART

determined to find the perfect spot. I wanted a table with a good view of the

canyon. Why was this so hard? If we were lucky, I might even get to see _____
                                                                       ANIMAL

eating some _____ on the cliffside. They don't have those in _____ where I
            PLURAL FRUIT   PLACE

am from. I walked down a little hill and there it was, the perfect spot! The trees

towered overhead and looked as tall as _____. The patch of grass was a
                                       SOMETHING TALL

beautiful _____ color. The _____ flowers were growing on
          COLOR   ADJECTIVE

the side of a _____. I looked across the canyon edge and even saw a
              NOUN

_____ on the edge of a rock. I looked back to see my _____ and
DIFFERENT ANIMAL   FAMILY MEMBER #1

_____ _____ a picnic basket. "I hope you brought plenty of
FAMILY MEMBER #2 VERB THAT ENDS IN ING

_____, I'm starving!"
A DIFFERENT FOOD

25

Hike Down to Havasupai Falls

DID YOU KNOW? You can visit the Havasupai Reservation and see their beautiful Havasupai Falls, a blue-green waterfall.

Phantom Ranch Word Search

Phantom Ranch is a special place at the bottom of the Grand Canyon. You can spend the night, relax, and get a hot meal. The lodge was designed by architect Mary Colter. It can only be reached by mule, hiking, or rafting the Colorado River.

1. dorms
2. cabins
3. canteen
4. mulerider
5. popular
6. oasis
7. rafters
8. bottom
9. sacred
10. hiking
11. descend
12. water
13. Mary Colter
14. backpackers
15. postcard
16. camping
17. stars
18. mule train
19. overnight
20. rest

```
F M R E S T O M B S T O N D S
E O I D P W A T E R B R N A N
G W C O M P S N B A E E K T G
R J T R L R I F L T C B U H K
A A E M R E S T E S A P W G P
V J D S S R T D E A N A L I S
P O P U L A R D B E T D S N B
R L M A R Y C O L T E R I R A
A T A T M D L E S E E R W E C
F S M U L E T R A I N R O V K
T G P A S R R D R A C T S O P
E N A H I C R G R H I U A K A
R I O W I A T O I B T R M C C
S P A H R S C K N N M O N P K
S M U L E R I D E R T N A L E
I A H V V N H S O T R A Q O R
O C O T G D E E O O O R V W S
N W X A K C A B I N S O H E M
```

27

Leave No Trace Quiz

Leave No Trace is a concept that helps people make decisions during outdoor recreation that protects the environment. There are seven principles that guide us when we spend time outdoors, whether you are in a national park or not. Are you an expert in Leave No Trace? Take this quiz and find out!

1. How can you plan ahead and prepare to ensure you have the best experience you can in the national park?
   a. Make sure you stop by the ranger station for a map and to ask about current conditions.
   b. Just wing it! You will know the best trail when you see it.
   c. Stick to your plan, even if conditions change. You traveled a long way to get here, and you should stick to your plan.
2. What is an example of traveling on a durable surface?
   a. Walking only on the designated path.
   b. Walking on the grass that borders the trail if the trail is very muddy.
   c. Taking a shortcut if you can find one because it means you will be walking less.
3. Why should you dispose of waste properly?
   a. You don't need to. Park rangers love to pick up the trash you leave behind.
   b. You should actually leave your leftovers behind, because animals will eat them. It is important to make sure they aren't hungry.
   c. So that other peoples' experiences of the park are not impacted by you leaving your waste behind.
4. How can you best follow the concept "leave what you find?"
   a. Take only a small rock or leaf to remember your trip.
   b. Take pictures, but leave any physical items where they are.
   c. Leave everything you find, unless it may be rare like an arrowhead, then it is okay to take.
5. What is not a good example of minimizing campfire impacts?
   a. Only having a campfire in a pre-existing campfire ring.
   b. Checking in with current conditions when you consider making a campfire.
   c. Building a new campfire ring in a location that has a better view.
6. What is a poor example of respecting wildlife?
   a. Building squirrel houses out of rocks so the squirrels have a place to live.
   b. Stay far away from wildlife and give them plenty of space.
   c. Reminding your grown-ups not to drive too fast in animal habitats while visiting the park.
7. How can you show consideration of other visitors?
   a. Play music on your speaker so other people at the campground can enjoy it.
   b. Wear headphones on the trail if you choose to listen to music.
   c. Make sure to yell "Hello!" to every animal you see at top volume.

Park Poetry

America's parks inspire art of all kinds. Painters, sculptors, photographers, writers, and artists of all mediums have taken inspiration from natural beauty. They have turned their inspiration into great works.

Use this space to write your own poem about the park. Think about what you have experienced or seen. Use descriptive language to create an acrostic poem. This type of poem has the first letter of each line spell out another word. Create an acrostic that spells out the word "Grand."

G _____

R _____

A _____

N _____

D _____

Great Wonder
Rainbow palette
Astronomical view
Never so vast
Deep into the earth

Gila Monsters
Red Rocks
Arizona
Navajo Bridge
Desert View

Rafting Down the Colorado

start here

Hop on a raft and make it to the end of the river.

DID YOU KNOW? Over 20,000 people go rafting on the Colorado River at the bottom of the canyon every year, including kids! If you had the chance, would you do it?

Stacking Rocks

Have you ever seen stacks of rocks while hiking in national parks? Do you know what they are or what they mean? These rock piles are called cairns and often mark hiking routes in parks. Every park has a different way to maintain trails and cairns. However, they all have the same rule: If you come across a cairn, do not disturb it!

Color the cairn and the rules to remember.

1. Do not tamper with cairns.

If a cairn is tampered with or an unauthorized one is built, then future visitors may become disoriented or even lost.

2. Do not build unauthorized cairns.

Moving rocks disturbs the soil and makes the area more prone to erosion. Disturbing rocks can disturb fragile plants.

3. Do not add to existing cairns.

Authorized cairns are carefully designed. Adding to them can actually cause them to collapse.

Crack the Code

Use the code to figure out some fun facts about Grand Canyon National Park.

ANSWER: A B C D E F G H I J K L M N O P Q R S T U V W Y
CODE: O T D A J K E F Y L R Q S W I G N H P U V M C B

What is the most popular pack animal in the park?

S V Q J P

The Grand Canyon is one of these famous places:

P J M J W   C I W A J H P
I K   U F J   C I H Q A

Some of the rocks at the bottom of the Grand Canyon are this old:

U C I   T Y Q Q Y I W

32

The Land of the Havasupai

There are eleven current tribes that have connections to the lands and resources now found within Grand Canyon National Park. The Havasupai Tribe is just one of those groups. The Tribe has a reservation at the bottom of the Grand Canyon. Complete the crossword puzzle below to learn more about the Havasupai people.

Word Bank

BLUE-GREEN
MULE TRAIN
AGRICULTURE
CORN
EIGHT MILES
SUPAI
TOURISM
CULTURE
ARIZONA
SILVER
HUNTING
ARTHUR
ART

Down

1. Modern-day state where most Havasupai people live
2. You can get to the village either by foot or this
5. The cultivating of the soil and production of crops
7. This precious metal was discovered by prospectors and brought unwelcomed people to Havasupai land
8. The American President that took traditional lands away from the Havasupai
9. Creative activities that express imaginative or technical skill. It produces a product or an object

Across

3. Main source of income for the Havasupai Tribe from people visiting their land
4. Killing things like sheep, deer, and rabbits for food
6. Distance from the canyon rim to the village
7. Town in Arizona where many Havasupai people live
10. Traditional crop grown by the Havasupai
11. This is ever-evolving and includes the customs, arts, social institutions, and achievements of a people group
12. Havasupai means "People of the ____-_____ waters"

33

Take a Mule Ride Down the Canyon

start here →

DID YOU KNOW?
You can camp at the bottom of the canyon. Phantom Ranch is an oasis with cabins or you can pitch a tent at the nearby Bright Angel Campground.

A Hike at the Grand Cayon

Fill in the blanks on this page without looking at the full story. Once you have each line filled out, use the words you've chosen to complete the story on the next page.

ADJECTIVE _____

SOMETHING TO EAT _____

SOMETHING TO DRINK _____

NOUN _____

ARTICLE OF CLOTHING _____

BODY PART _____

VERB _____

ANIMAL _____

SAME TYPE OF FOOD _____

ADJECTIVE _____

SAME ANIMAL _____

VERB THAT ENDS IN "ED" _____

NUMBER _____

A DIFFERENT NUMBER _____

SOMETHING THAT FLIES _____

LIGHT SOURCE _____

PLURAL NOUN _____

FAMILY MEMBER _____

YOUR NICKNAME _____

A Hike at the Grand Canyon

Use the words from the previous page to complete a silly story.

I went for a hike at the Grand Canyon today. In my favorite _____
                                                              ADJECTIVE

backpack, I made sure to pack a map so I wouldn't get lost. I also threw in an

extra _____ just in case I got hungry and a bottle of _____.
      SOMETHING TO EAT   SOMETHING TO DRINK

I put on my _____ spray, and I tied a _____ around my
            NOUN   ARTICLE OF CLOTHING

_____, in case it gets chilly. I started to _____ down the path. As
BODY PART   VERB

soon as I turned the corner, I came face to face with a(n) _____. I think
                                                           ANIMAL

it was as startled as I was! What should I do? I had to think fast! Should I

give it some of my _____? No. I had to remember what the
                   SAME TYPE OF FOOD

_____ ranger told me: "If you see one, back away slowly and try not to
ADJECTIVE

scare it." Soon enough, the _____ _____ away. The coast
                            SAME ANIMAL   VERB THAT ENDS IN ED

was clear. _____ hours later, I finally got to the lookout. I felt like I could
           NUMBER

see for a _____ miles across the canyon. I took a picture of a _____ so
          A DIFFERENT NUMBER   NOUN

I could always remember this moment. As I was putting my camera away, a

_____ flew by, reminding me that it was almost nighttime. I turned on
SOMETHING THAT FLIES

my _____ and headed back. I could hear the _____ singing
   LIGHT SOURCE   PLURAL INSECT

their evening song. Just as I was getting tired, I saw my _____ and
                                                          FAMILY MEMBER

our tent. "Welcome back _____! How was your hike?"
                        NICKNAME

Let's Go Camping Word Search

Words may be horizontal, vertical, diagonal, or they might be backwards!

1. tent
2. camp stove
3. sleeping bag
4. bug spray
5. sunscreen
6. map
7. flashlight
8. pillow
9. lantern
10. ice
11. snacks
12. smores
13. water
14. first aid kit
15. chair
16. cards
17. books
18. games
19. trail
20. hat

```
D P P I L L O W D B T E A C I
E O A D P R E A A M B R C A N
P W C A M P S T O V E I H X G
R A H S G E L E B E E D A P S
E L B U G S P R A Y N G I E A
S I A H G C I C N N M E R C N
C W N L A F I R S K O O B F K
M T A E M I L E L H M R W L J
T A P R E A O R E S L B A A B
S M P A S R R T E N T L U S C
C E A I I R C G P E I U J H A
S S N A C K S S I M O K I L R
I J R S F O I S N J R A Q I D
C Y E T L E V E G U O R V G S
E W T A K C A B B S O H H M
X J N F I R S T A I D K I T T
U A A E S S E N G E T P V A B
C J L I A R T D N A M A H A S
```

All in the Day of a Park Ranger

Park Rangers are hardworking individuals dedicated to protecting our parks, monuments, museums, and more. They take care of the natural and cultural resources for future generations. Rangers also help protect the visitors of the park. Their responsibilities are broad and they work both with the public and behind the scenes.

What have you seen park rangers do? Use your knowledge of the duties of park rangers to fill out a typical daily schedule, listing one activity for each hour. Feel free to make up your own, but some examples of activities are provided on the right. Read carefully! Not all the example activities are befitting a ranger.

6 am	Lead a sunrise hike
7 am	
8 am	
9 am	
10 am	
11 am	
12 pm	Enjoy a lunch break outside
1 pm	
2 pm	
3 pm	
4 pm	Teach visitors about the geology of the canyon
5 pm	
6 pm	
7 pm	
8 pm	
9 pm	

- feed the condors
- build trails for visitors to enjoy
- throw rocks off the side of the canyon
- rescue lost hikers
- study animal behavior
- record air quality data
- answer questions at the visitor center
- pick wildflowers
- pick up litter
- share marshmallows with squirrels
- repair handrails
- lead a class on a field trip
- catch toads and make them race
- lead people on educational hikes
- write articles for the park website
- protect the river from pollution
- remove non-native plants from the park
- study how climate change is affecting the park
- give a talk about mountain lions
- lead a program for campers on erosion

If you were a park ranger, which of the above tasks would you enjoy most?

_____

_____

Draw Yourself as a Park Ranger

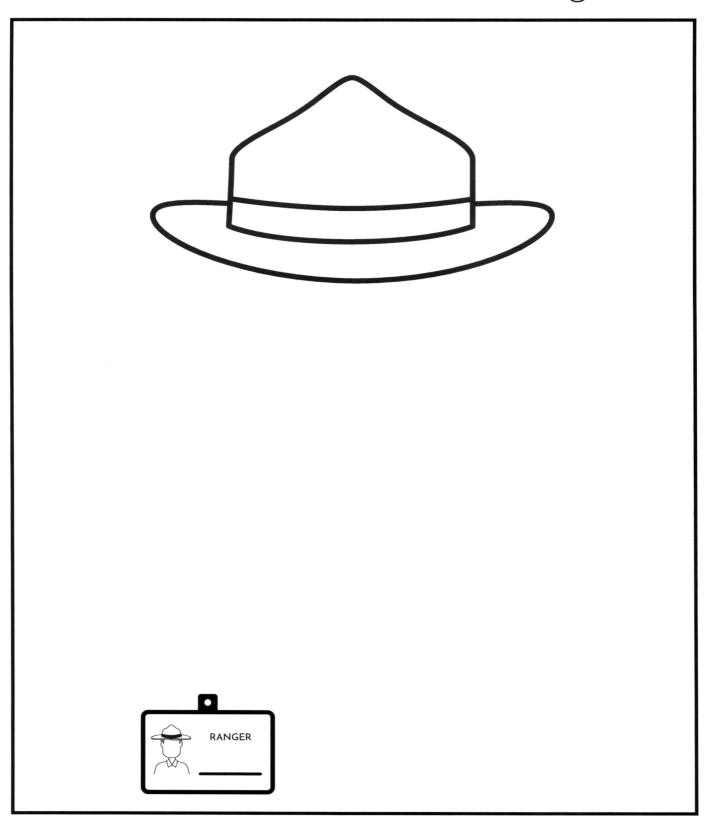

Rattlesnakes of the Grand Canyon

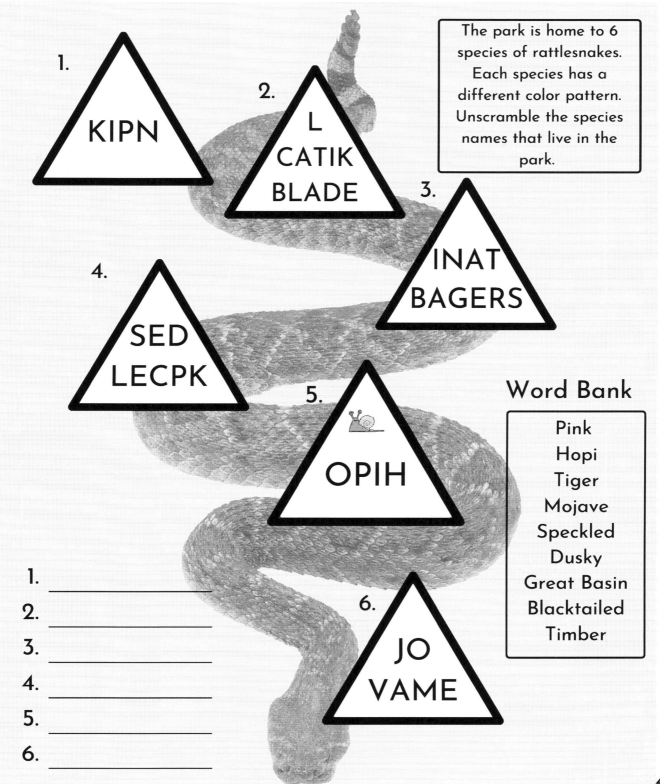

The park is home to 6 species of rattlesnakes. Each species has a different color pattern. Unscramble the species names that live in the park.

1. KIPN
2. L CATIK BLADE
3. INAT BAGERS
4. SED LECPK
5. OPIH
6. JO VAME

Word Bank

Pink
Hopi
Tiger
Mojave
Speckled
Dusky
Great Basin
Blacktailed
Timber

1. _____
2. _____
3. _____
4. _____
5. _____
6. _____

Amphibians

Four species of toads and two species of frogs live in the Grand Canyon. Frogs and toads both spend the beginning of their lives the same way - as tadpoles. Tadpoles hatch from eggs, usually in springs or pools of water.

Both frogs and toads are amphibians. Color the amphibians below.

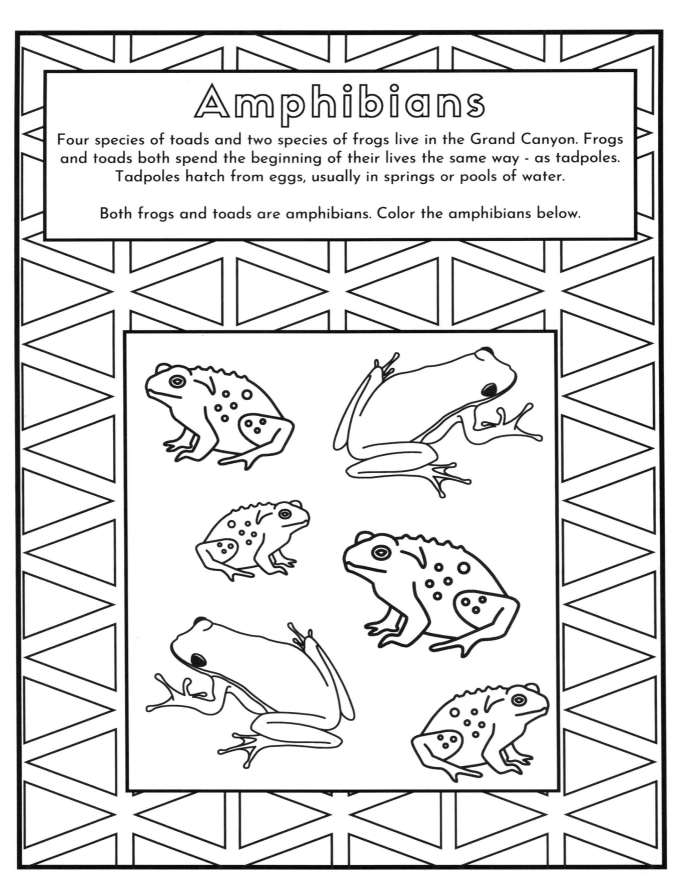

63 National Parks

How many other national parks have you been to? Which one do you want to visit next? Note that some of these parks fall on the border of more than one state, you may check it off more than once!

Alaska
- [ ] Denali National Park
- [ ] Gates of the Arctic National Park
- [ ] Glacier Bay National Park
- [ ] Katmai National Park
- [ ] Kenai Fjords National Park
- [ ] Kobuk Valley National Park
- [ ] Lake Clark National Park
- [ ] Wrangell-St. Elias National Park

American Samoa
- [ ] National Park of American Samoa

Arizona
- [ ] Grand Canyon National Park
- [ ] Petrified Forest National Park
- [ ] Saguaro National Park

Arkansas
- [ ] Hot Springs National Park

California
- [ ] Channel Islands National Park
- [ ] Death Valley National Park
- [ ] Joshua Tree National Park
- [ ] Kings Canyon National Park
- [ ] Lassen Volcanic National Park
- [ ] Pinnacles National Park
- [ ] Redwood National Park
- [ ] Sequoia National Park
- [ ] Yosemite National Park

Colorado
- [ ] Black Canyon of the Gunnison National Park
- [ ] Great Sand Dunes National Park
- [ ] Mesa Verde National Park
- [ ] Rocky Mountain National Park

Florida
- [ ] Biscayne National Park
- [ ] Dry Tortugas National Park
- [ ] Everglades National Park

Hawaii
- [ ] Haleakala National Park
- [ ] Hawai'i Volcanoes National Park

Idaho
- [ ] Yellowstone National Park

Kentucky
- [ ] Mammoth Cave National Park

Indiana
- [ ] Indiana Dunes National Park

Maine
- [ ] Acadia National Park

Michigan
- [ ] Isle Royale National Park

Minnesota
- [ ] Voyageurs National Park

Missouri
- [ ] Gateway Arch National Park

Montana
- [ ] Glacier National Park
- [ ] Yellowstone National Park

Nevada
- [ ] Death Valley National Park
- [ ] Great Basin National Park

New Mexico
- [ ] Carlsbad Caverns National Park
- [ ] White Sands National Park

North Dakota
- [ ] Theodore Roosevelt National Park

North Carolina
- [ ] Great Smoky Mountains National Park

Ohio
- [ ] Cuyahoga Valley National Park

Oregon
- [ ] Crater Lake National Park

South Carolina
- [ ] Congaree National Park

South Dakota
- [ ] Badlands National Park
- [ ] Wind Cave National Park

Tennessee
- [ ] Great Smoky Mountains National Park

Texas
- [ ] Big Bend National Park
- [ ] Guadalupe Mountains National Park

Utah
- [ ] Arches National Park
- [ ] Bryce Canyon National Park
- [ ] Canyonlands National Park
- [ ] Capitol Reef National Park
- [ ] Zion National Park

Virgin Islands
- [ ] Virgin Islands National Park

Virginia
- [ ] Shenandoah National Park

Washington
- [ ] Mount Rainier National Park
- [ ] North Cascades National Park
- [ ] Olympic National Park

West Virginia
- [ ] New River Gorge National Park

Wyoming
- [ ] Grand Teton National Park
- [ ] Yellowstone National Park

Other National Parks Crossword

Besides Grand Canyon National Park, there are 62 other diverse and beautiful national parks across the United States. Try your hand at this crossword. If you need help, look at the previous page for some hints.

Down

1. State where Acadia National Park is located
2. This national park has the Spanish word for turtle in it
3. Number of national parks in Alaska
5. This national park has some of the hottest temperatures in the world
6. This national park is the only one in Idaho
7. This toothsome creature can famously be found in Everglades National Park
8. Only president with a national park named for them

Across

4. This state has the most national parks
9. This park has some of the newest land in the US, caused by volcanic eruptions
10. This park has the deepest lake in the United States
11. This color shows up in the name of a national park in California
12. This national park deserves a gold medal

Which National Park Will You Go To Next? Word Search

1. Zion
2. Big Bend
3. Glacier
4. Olympic
5. Sequoia
6. Bryce
7. Mesa Verde
8. Biscayne
9. Wind Cave
10. Great Basin
11. Katmai
12. Yellowstone
13. Voyageurs
14. Arches
15. Badlands
16. Denali
17. Glacier Bay
18. Hot Springs

```
F M M E S A V E R D E B N E Y
E A B I G B E N D E S A S E M
Y L I C A L O Y N E E D L T G
D M G A S S A U C N R L U E R
C E L I I T S C R E O A A K E
S N A W Y E E O I W T N A C A
G I C H A A Q C S E M D N S T
N O I Z P R U T I M R S N E B
I W E L M P O N B W E B K H A
R J R F D N I F L I H B U C S
P A B E E S A N E S O P W R I
S J A E N Y A C S I B A U A N
T C Y I A D O H H Y M E A L R
O T A T L M L E S E G R W R J
H S T O I K A T M A I R O P B
I C H U R C O L Y M P I C O U
O Y G T S D E O S B R Y C E T
W I N D C A V E I N R O H E M
```

45

ANSWER KEY

Answers: Who Lives Here?

Here are eleven plants and animals that live in the park.
Use the word bank to fill in the clues below.

word bank: javelina, mountain lion, ringtail, condor, falcon, gila monster, rattlesnake, tarantula, utah yucca, burrobush, salt cedar

RINGTAIL

BURROBUSH

TARANTULA

MOUNTAIN LION

CONDOR

SALT CEDAR

GILA MONSTER

RATTLESNAKE

UTAH YUCCA

FALCON

JAVELINA

47

Find the Match!
Common Names and Latin Names

Match the common name to the scientific name for each animal. The first one is done for you. Use clues on the page before and after this one to complete the matches.

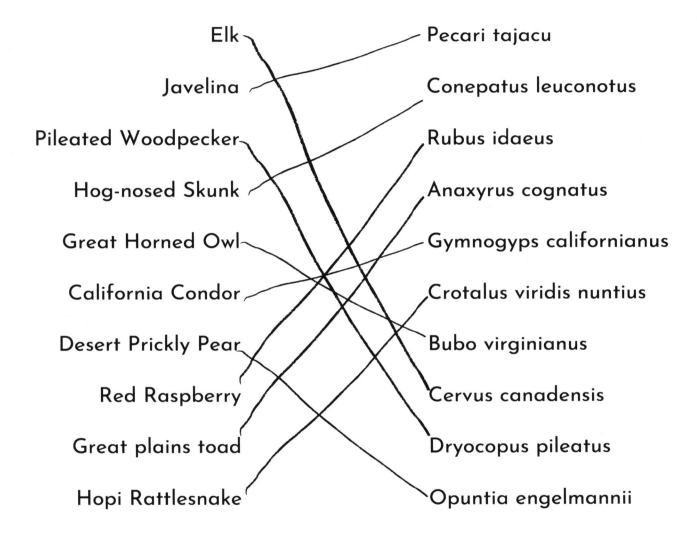

Answers: The Ten Essentials

The ten essentials are a list of things that are important to have when you go for longer hikes. If you go on a hike to the <u>backcountry</u>, it is especially important that you have everything you need in case of an emergency. If you get lost or something unforeseen happens, it is good to be prepared to survive until help finds you.

The ten essentials list was developed in the 1930s by an outdoors group called the Mountaineers. Over time and technological advancements, this list has evolved. Can you identify all the things on the current list? Circle each of the "essentials" and cross out everything that doesn't make the cut.

Backcountry- a remote undeveloped rural area.

Jumbles Answers

Unscramble the letters to uncovering activities you can do while in Grand Canyon National Park. Hint: each one ends in -ing.

1. RAFTING
2. HIKING
3. BIRDING
4. CAMPING
5. PICNICKING
6. SIGHTSEEING
7. MULERIDING

Go Birdwatching for the California Condor

DID YOU KNOW? The California Condor almost went extinct? In 1982, there were less than 30 California Condors left in the world.

Grand Canyon Word Search

1. Arizona
2. Colorado River
3. bats
4. condor
5. Hopi
6. deep
7. rodents
8. Navajo
9. mule
10. rafting
11. Havasupai
12. fungi
13. Paiute
14. Hualapai
15. rapids
16. geology
17. helicopters
18. erosion
19. South Rim
20. North Rim

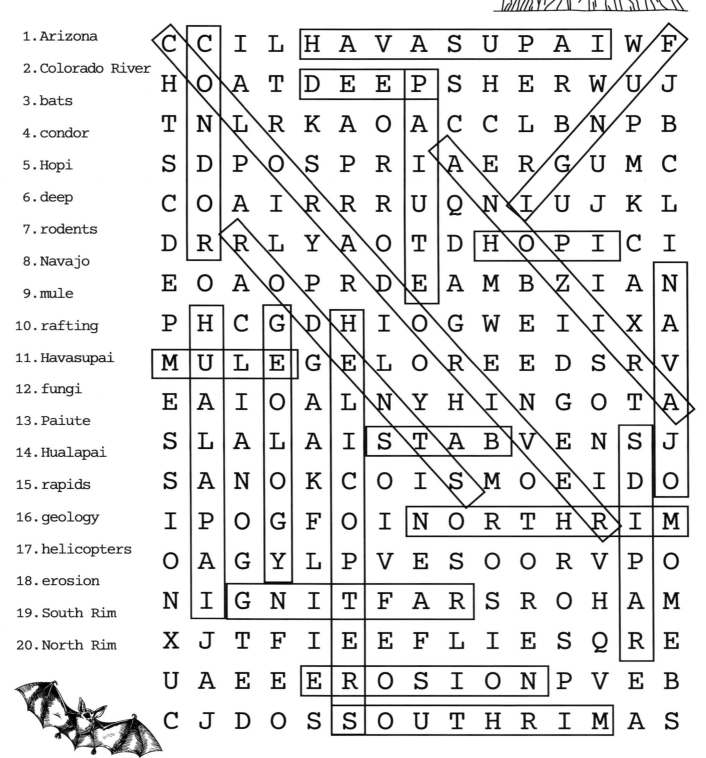

Answers: Find the Match!
What are Baby Animals Called?

Match the animal to its baby. The first one is done for you.

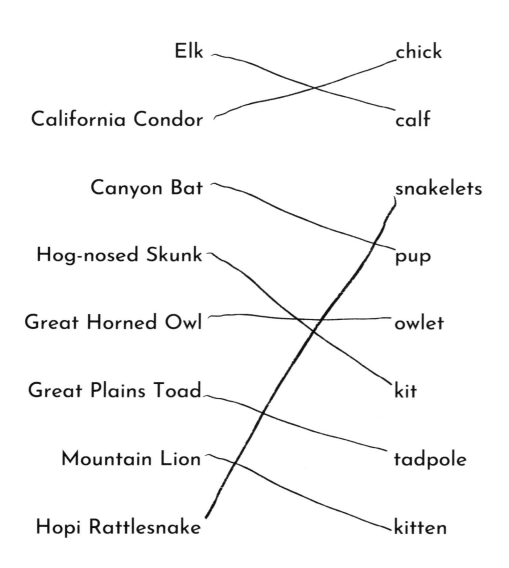

53

Crack the Code

Use the code to figure out some fun facts about Grand Canyon National Park

ANSWER: A B C D E F G H I J K L M N O P Q R S T U V W Y
CODE: O T D A J K E F Y L R Q S W I G N H P U V M C B

What is the most popular pack animal in the park?

M U L E S
S V Q J P

The Grand Canyon is one of these famous places:

S E V E N   W O N D E R S
P J M J W   C I W A J H P

O F   T H E   W O R L D
I K   U F J   C I H Q A

Some of the rocks at the bottom of the Grand Canyon are this old:

T W O   B I L L I O N
U C I   T Y Q Q Y I W

Hike Down to Havasupai Falls

DID YOU KNOW? You can visit the Havasupai Reservation and see their beautiful Havasupai Falls, a blue-green waterfall.

Phantom Ranch Word Search

Phantom Ranch is a special place at the bottom of the Grand Canyon. You can spend the night, relax, and get a hot meal. The lodge was designed by architect Mary Colter. It can only be reached by mule, hiking, or rafting the Colorado River.

1. dorms
2. cabins
3. canteen
4. mulerider
5. popular
6. oasis
7. rafters
8. bottom
9. sacred
10. hiking
11. descend
12. water
13. Mary Colter
14. backpackers
15. postcard
16. camping
17. stars
18. mule train
19. overnight
20. rest

```
F M R E S T O M B S T O N D S
E O I D P W A T E R B R N A N
G W C O M P S N B A E E K T G
R J T R L R I F L T C B U H K
A A E M R E S T E S A P W G P
V J D S S R T D E A N A L I S
P O P U L A R D B E T D S N B
R L M A R Y C O L T E R I R A
A T A T M D L E S E E R W E C
F S M U L E T R A I N R O V K
T G P A S R R D R A C T S O P
E N A H I C R G R H I U A K A
R I O W I A T O I B T R M C C
S P A H R S C K N N M O N P K
S M U L E R I D E R T N A L E
I A H V V N H S O T R A Q O R
O C O T G D E E O O R V W S
N W X A K C A B I N S O H E M
```

Solution: Rafting Down the Colorado

Hop on a raft and make it to the end of the river.

DID YOU KNOW?
Over 20,000 people go rafting on the Colorado River at the bottom of the canyon every year, including kids! If you had the chance, would you do it?

Answers: Leave No Trace Quiz

Leave No Trace is a concept that helps people make decisions during outdoor recreation that protects the environment. There are seven principles that guide us when we spend time outdoors, whether you are in a national park or not. Are you an expert in Leave No Trace? Take this quiz and find out!

1. How can you plan ahead and prepare to ensure you have the best experience you can in the National Park?
    A. Make sure you stop by the ranger station for a map and to ask about current conditions.
2. What is an example of traveling on a durable surface?
    A. Walking only on the designated path.
3. Why should you dispose of waste properly?
    C. So that other peoples' experiences of the park are not impacted by you leaving your waste behind.
4. How can you best follow the concept "leave what you find?"
    B. Take pictures but leave any physical items where they are.
5. What is not a good example of minimizing campfire impacts?
    C. Building a new campfire ring in a location that has a better view.
6. What is a poor example of respecting wildlife?
    A. Building squirrel houses out of rocks from the river so the squirrels have a place to live.
7. How can you show consideration of other visitors?
    B. Wear headphones on the trail if you choose to listen to music.

The Land of the Havasupai

There are eleven current tribes that have connections to the lands and resources now found within Grand Canyon National Park. The Havasupai Tribe is just one of those groups. The Tribe has a reservation at the bottom of the Grand Canyon. Complete the crossword puzzle below to learn more about the Havasupai people.

Word Bank

BLUE-GREEN
MULE TRAIN
AGRICULTURE
CORN
EIGHT MILES
SUPAI
TOURISM
CULTURE
ARIZONA
SILVER
HUNTING
ARTHUR
ART

Down

1. Modern-day state where most Havasupai people live
2. You can get to the village either by foot or this
5. The cultivating of the soil and production of crops
7. This precious metal was discovered by prospectors and brought unwelcomed people to Havasupai land
8. The American President that took traditional lands away from the Havasupai
9. Creative activities that express imaginative or technical skill. It produces a product, an object

Across

3. Main source of income for the Havasupai Tribe from people visiting their land
4. Killing things like sheep, deer, and rabbits for food
6. Distance from the canyon rim to the village
7. Town in Arizona where many Havasupai people live
10. Traditional crop grown by the Havasupai
11. This is ever-evolving and includes the customs, arts, social institutions, and achievements of a people group
12. Havasupai means "People of the ____-_____ waters"

Solution: Take a Mule Ride Down the Canyon

DID YOU KNOW? You can camp at the bottom of the canyon. Phantom Ranch is an oasis with cabins or you can pitch a tent at the nearby Bright Angel Campground

Let's Go Camping Word Search

1. tent
2. camp stove
3. sleeping bag
4. bug spray
5. sunscreen
6. map
7. flashlight
8. pillow
9. lantern
10. ice
11. snacks
12. smores
13. water
14. first aid kit
15. chair
16. cards
17. books
18. games
19. trail
20. hat

```
D P P I L L O W D B T E A C I
E O A D P R E A A M B R C A N
P W C A M P S T O V E I H X G
R A H S G E L E B E E D A P S
E L B U G S P R A Y N G I E A
S I A H G C I C N N M E R C N
C W N L A F I R S K O O B F K
M T A E M I L E L H M R W L J
T A P R E A O R E S L B A A B
S M P A S R R T E N T L U S C
C E A I I R C G P E I U J H A
S S N A C K S S I M O K I L R
I J R S F O I S N J R A Q I D
C Y E T L E V E G U O R V G S
E W T A K C A B B S S O H H M
X J N F I R S T A I D K I T T
U A A E S S E N G E T P V A B
C J L I A R T D N A M A H A S
```

All in the Day of a Park Ranger

There are many right answers for this activity, but not all of the provided examples are good activities for a park ranger. In fact, a park ranger's job may include stopping visitors from doing some of these things.

The list below are activities that rangers do not do:

feed the condors

throw rocks off the side of the canyon

pick wildflowers

share marshmallows with squirrels

catch toads and make them race

Solution:
Rattlesnakes of the Grand Canyon

1. PINK
2. BLACKTAILED
3. GREAT BASIN
4. SPECKLED
5. HOPI
6. MOJAVE

Answers: Other National Parks

Besides Grand Canyon National Park, there are 62 other diverse and beautiful national parks across the United States. Try your hand at this crossword. If you need help, look at the previous page for some hints.

Down

1. State where Acadia National Park is located
2. This National Park has the Spanish word for turtle in it
3. Number of National Parks in Alaska
5. This National Park has some of the hottest temperatures in the world
6. This National Park is the only one in Idaho
7. This toothsome creature can famously be found in Everglades National Park
8. Only president with a national park named for them

Across

4. This state has the most National Parks
9. This park has some of the newest land in the US, caused by a volcanic eruption
10. This park has the deepest lake in the United States
11. This color shows up in the name of a National Park in California
12. This National Park deserves a gold medal

Answers: Which National Park Will You Go To Next?

1. Zion
2. Big Bend
3. Glacier
4. Olympic
5. Sequoia
6. Bryce
7. Mesa Verde
8. Biscayne
9. Wind Cave
10. Great Basin
11. Katmai
12. Yellowstone
13. Voyageurs
14. Arches
15. Badlands
16. Denali
17. Glacier Bay
18. Hot Springs

Little Bison Press is an independent children's book publisher based in the Pacific Northwest. We promote exploration, conservation, and adventure through our books. Established in 2021, our passion for outside spaces and travel inspired the creation of Little Bison Press.

We seek to publish books that support children in learning about and caring for the natural places in our world.

To learn more, visit:
www.littlebisonpress.com